How To Piss Off A Salesman

SIDNEY S. PRASAD

ISBN:1927676355
ISBN-13: 978-1-927676-35-6

DEDICATION

This book is dedicated to my dear parents. Thank you for completing my world.

CONTENTS

ACKNOWLEDGMENTS

Hi my name is Sidney S. Prasad and I'm going to teach you over one hundred ways to defend yourself against a door-to-door salesman. I've spent over a decade in the field of selling. I have been involved with the promotion of small turnkey projects and promoting products and services of very large Fortune Five Hundred companies. I've worked with both brilliant sales professionals along with the slimiest scum on the face of this planet.

While working in the sales industry, I got the opportunity to attend several sales seminars, read countless selling books and learned all of the techniques on how to convince someone to sign on the dotted line. One day, I made a conscious decision to come back to your side and help innocent prospects fight back against those degenerate vultures that knock on the door. In fact, it's very rare an ex-sales professional will turn around and rat out the industry that fed him for a decade.

Please allow me to ask you the following questions:

Aren't you sick and tired of getting your dinner interrupted by some snake-oil-salesman who wants to see your natural gas bill?

If your current basic cable package meets your needs, then why should you waste your time listening to a sales pitch on switching to the deluxe package?

If an insider from the sales industry was willing to teach you on how to get rid of a pesky door-to-door salesman in roughly two minutes, wouldn't you be intrigued?

Between the evening commute home, grabbing a bite to eat, preparing for the next day, do you really have 10 minutes to spare and listen to a sales spiel?

It is evident when a consumer receives bad service they go and tell at least ten people about their negative experience. On the flip side whenever a prospect does something negative to a salesman they also go and share the story with their colleagues.

People let's fight back and get rid of those time wasting salespeople. Make a decision right now to never again get robbed of your valuable time by a scum bag, street hustling salesman. Get ready to hear about humorous things people have done and have dreamed about doing to piss off salesman!

1 NOW WE ARE EVEN!

Listen to the sales presentation and repeat everything verbatim that the salesman is telling you.

Take your clothes off and answer the door nude.

Answer the door and pretend that you can't hear. Only communicate with your hands.

Wet your hands prior to answering the door and only listen to half of the sales presentation. Then say, "Oh shit I pissed on my hands again." Then flick your wet hands towards the salesman's face.

Answer the door and pretend that you are a prostitute. Ask the salesman if they are looking for some company.

Listen to the salesman's questions and answer back in a foreign language.

Open the door and continuously take pictures of the salesman.

Open the door and boldly ask the salesman if this is his sick idea of a knock knock joke. Then slam the door before he can answer you.

Don't answer the door, but violently start knocking on the other side of the door.

Kindly tell the salesman that you are getting evicted in two days and moving to the streets.

Open the door and tape a "Absolutely No Solicitors, Peddlers or Agents Allowed" sign.

Listen to the salesman's questions and answer back stuttering really badly.

Engage in a conversation with the salesman but talk extremely slow and pause frequently.

Answer the door with a ski mask on and tell them that you are in the middle of a robbery.

Answer the door with a couple of boxes in your hand. Then ask the salesman if he will help you move.

Listen to the first minute of the sales presentation and then interrupt the salesman. Tell him that you thought he was the pizza delivery guy. Excuse yourself from the conversation and say you got to go call the pizza parlor and find out what happened to your dinner.

Open the door and take the salesman's clipboard and fart on it. Then slam the door before one of you break out in laughter.

Open the door and start acting like a mime.

Listen to the sales presentation while passionately scratching your crotch area.

Answer the door with a megaphone and say, "Get out!"

While the salesman is delivering their presentation, break out into an exercise routine. Do a couple of jumping jacks, push-ups and abdominal crunches.

Interrupt the sales presentation and repeatedly ask questions about the return policy.

Listen to the sales pitch and ask the salesman if it's their first day because they sound really shitty.

Fill a condom with water and throw it at the salesman from an upstairs window.

Open the door and scream as loud as you can.

Ask the salesman for their home address. Then tell them you will knock on their door during dinner time to listen to their pitch.

Listen to the sales spiel in its entirety and then say the following phrases:

"Say what now?"

"Come again?"

"Huh?"

Continuously open and close the door until they go away.

Put some meat on your front porch and let your dog loose.

Go outside and turn your sprinkler on in the direction of the salesman.

Pick your nose as you listen to the sales presentation and then pull something out and wipe it on the salesman.

Stick a lighter by your smoke detector and make your fire alarm go off prior to answering the door. Then run outside, waving your arms and yell, "fire."

Listen to the sales pitch and keep saying, "No," like a broken record.

Grab a basket of dirty laundry and hand it to the salesman. Tell them to have it washed and pressed by Saturday and then close the door.

Answer the door and pull the salesman's pants down. Pray they are not rolling commando.

Open the door, get outside and lock it. Then get in your car and drive away.

Open the door and scream, "pervert, rape, sicko," at the top of your lungs.

Answer the door and ask the salesman if they came for the strip poker game.

Don't open your door but start flicking your porch light on and off until they leave.

Listen to half of the sales speech and pretend that you have tourette's syndrome. Loudly swear obscenities and then switch back to normal mode simultaneously.

Ignore the salesman, go outside and start cutting your lawn.

Ask the salesman if they have an appointment to see you. There is a 99.9% chance they will say no and then slam the door on them.

Go outside and jog away.

Regardless of how old you are tell the salesman that you are under 18 and not legally qualified to make a purchasing decision.

If you spot a salesman coming in towards your house, then rub some dog crap on your door bell to deter them.

Grab some makeup and pretend that you are the Avon lady. Before the salesman can talk, start pitching them on Avon.

Open your door and unscrew the porch light bulb, then go back inside the house.

Answer the door and start exotically grinding the salesman.

While you are listening to the sales presentation, stick your hand inside your pants and start feeling yourself.

Don't answer the door but shoot a toy cap gun from the other side of the door. This will make them poop their pants.

Open the door and put a screaming baby in the salesman's hands.

Crank your stereo as loud as possible prior to answering the door. During the presentation tell the salesman that you can't make out what they are saying.

Tell the salesman that you just got evicted and are in the middle of vacating the property.

Open the door and start crying like a little bitch. Hold on to the salesman and get them to console you.

Answer the door and accuse the salesman of being a collector. Tell them that you aren't going to pay your bill and slam the door shut.

Wait for the salesman to start talking then say, "Shhh." Then gently close the door on them.

Open the door with a rope tied around your neck and say, "Life sucks."

Listen to the entire sales presentation then clap your hands and close the door.

As the salesman delivers his pitch move close to him to the point where your noses are almost touching.

Open the door and don't say a word. Then take the mailbox off its hinges and take it back with you inside the house.

Answer the door with an empty pillow case in your hands and say, "Trick or treat."

Don't answer the door but yell,
"Help" from the other side.

Don't answer the door but keep opening and closing your blinds.

Open the door and quickly flash the salesman and then shut the door.

Interrupt the sales spiel and tell the salesman that you only shop online.

If some kids are trying to sell you cookies, then tell them that you are a vegan and there are eggs inside the cookies.

If some kids are trying to sell you chocolate almonds, then tell them that you are diabetic.

Answer the door and identify yourself as a maid or butler. Then tell the salesman that the residents of the house are gone away on a 6 month world tour.

Open the door and don't say a word but just keep smiling.

Go into a rant and blatantly accuse the salesman of stealing your newspaper.

Pretend to be an undercover detective and disclaim that you are investigating a murder scene.

Go outside and lie down on the driveway and play dead.

Open the door and moon the salesman.

Listen to the sales presentation and start asking your imaginary spouse for input.

Open the door and say, "hello" then say "goodbye" and close the door.

Get into to your car and keep revving your engine until the salesman gives up and leaves.

Open the door while talking on your cell phone and continue talking until the salesman gives up and leaves.

Tell the salesman that they are trespassing and you are calling the Police.

Demand that the salesman takes you off their list or you will sue them.

Tell the salesman that you want their tie, clipboard and briefcase as a free sample.

Ask the salesman to quote you minus their commission or pay rate.

Answer the door in your boxer shorts and start playing with your nipples as the salesman talks.

Say "your mama" after everything the salesman says.

Each time the salesman asks you a question, answer back moaning like you are having sex.

Open the door holding a large kitchen knife dipped in ketchup.

Open the door from the chain and start barking like a dog.

Answer the door with your fly undone and part of your family jewels sticking out.

Kindly tell the salesman that you are pet sitting and don't know when the homeowners are back.

Pour spaghetti sauce all over your body and pretend that you are running from a murderer.

Ask the salesman for a piggyback ride around the block.

Ask the salesman if they are a pharmacy delivery person. Then explain to them that your psychiatrist arranged to get some Prozac and antidepressants delivered to you.

Go into a rant and accuse the salesman of having an affair with your significant other.

Wait for the salesman to present you with a question. Then say, "I can't tell you that but I can tell you my bank card pin number."

10 JOKES ON YOU

Answer the door and explain that you are a squatter.

Open a window and fling a pair of your soiled underwear at the salesman.

Tell the salesman you aren't allowed to speak to strangers and then slam the door.

Ask the salesman for some loose change and tell them that your social worker cut you off welfare.

Open the door and start flossing your teeth, don't say a thing and continue flossing.

Ask the salesman if they are the stripper your buddy hired for your stag party.

Go outside and urinate on your driveway, then go back inside your house.

Halfway during their presentation, pull your shirt over your head and ignore what they are telling you.

Ask the salesman if he will
help you clean your garage.

Continually ask a bunch of random, irrelevant questions to the salesman until he takes a hint and leaves.

Conclusion

In conclusion, I ask you, what would be the ultimate revenge to get even with those knuckled-headed salesmen? I ask myself that question every time when I barely escape choking on my dinner when a salesman knocks on my door. I sometimes fantasize about having unbreakable super glue on my door bell and trapping the salesman there until the end of winter.

I really wonder what would happen if a prospect lost their mind and decided to make an example out of the salesman. Would this result in a couple of Police cars getting dispatched? Then the prospect and the salesman would be stuck in the same jail cell together.

It wouldn't be astonishing to pick up a newspaper or hear a story one day on the nightly news about a salesman jumping off the roof of his office. Trust me. If the average person got the door slammed on them five thousand times, they would go insane too. Between the repetition of sales pitches and getting bitten by dogs every day, something's got give, right?

I'm not trying to say that all salesmen are slimy, as there are those rare individuals who will exit the premises as soon as the prospect announces that they are not interested. But I'm trying to make an example out of those low-lives that purposely won't take no for an answer.

Throughout this book, we covered typical high school pranks and some outrageously demented tactics. But there is one prank that would make the history books and get the prospect in serious crap. I can only see this getting executed on the big screen. I'm conceptualizing a prospect locating the harassing salesman's house. Then getting one hundred or more of their friends to simultaneously knock on the salesman's door every five minutes pretending to be a salesperson.

In a fantasy world, there are a million things a prospect can do to get their revenge on a salesman. Ranging from dumping maggots on the salesman's clipboard, pissing on their brief case and making a B.S. complaint to the authorities. But in reality, the prospect would be stooping to the salesman's level and could end up in jail or feeling really shitty for five minutes for doing something cruel.

As mentioned before, I wrote this book for pure entertainment for people who are sick of pesky salespeople. We all have a prankster living inside us dying to come out once in awhile but we are bounded by the laws of karma. For every action, there is a reaction some may believe. So even if you think you can get away with it, someone in a metaphysical sense is always watching and you can never go against the universe.

For what it's worth, if someone were to ask me what I personally think is the best revenge on a door-to-door salesman, it is very simple; don't answer the door. Most average salesmen would quit after the second no answer attempt. Or worse, they would give up on you and harass your neighbor. But imagine getting everyone in a ten mile radius to agree in not opening their door. The poor salesman would have to change his profession faster than you could flip over your soiled underwear.

ABOUT THE AUTHOR

Sidney S. Prasad is an author on a quest to make the world laugh. His work is focused on entertaining people with his dry-humored novels. Sidney S. Prasad personally believes laughter is the best cure for all of life's ups and downs.

Some other humorous books written by Sidney S. Prasad include:

How To Piss Off A Telemarketer,
Don't Ask Dumb Questions!
My Bipolar Manager,
The World's Biggest Piss Offs
Corny Names & Stupid Places,
Misfortune Cookies,
How To Irritate A Telemarketer
Plenty Of Freaks: Are You Sold On Online Dating?
Plenty Of Freaks: Worst Online Dating Mistakes
Plenty Of Freaks: Is Dating Legalized Prostitution?
and
Telemarketer's Revenge: The Customer Is Always Wrong, Bitch!